The Gift

A Tale of Adventure, Courage and Hope

Written by
Brent Coley

Illustrated by
Johnny Davis

The Gift:
A Tale of Adventure, Courage, and Hope

Written by Brent Coley
Illustrated by Johnny Davis

Published by BCB (Brent Coley Books)
Murrieta, CA

This is a work of fiction. Names, characters, events, and incidents are the products of the author's imagination. Any resemblance to actual persons, living or dead, or actual events is purely coincidental.

Decorative horizontal line courtesy of GDJ
https://www.needpix.com/photo/895645/

For more information about the author, visit
www.brentcoley.com

For more information about the illustrator, visit
www.storylandstudios.com

ISBN: 979-8-9856664-0-3

Dedication

For my children, Meghan and Ben –
You are my gifts from above.
May you continue to choose the right path,
even if it means walking alone.

The Castle of Byland

Map of Byland

The Dark Forest

Quinn's Village

Quinn

In a faraway land, deep within the kingdom of Byland, there was a small village. In it lived a boy. A boy named Quinn.

Like most twelve-year-old boys in the kingdom, he enjoyed riding horses, climbing trees, and hunting squirrels with his sling. But Quinn's life was different. He didn't have the one thing other boys and girls his age took for granted – a family.

Nine years earlier, just after his third birthday, Quinn's mother and father tragically passed away from a deadly fever that swept through the kingdom. Fortunately for Quinn, his uncle Erik took him in to raise as his own. This he did until war fell upon the land. Bound by his devotion to the king, Erik answered the call for soldiers. He left Quinn in the care of Judith and Henry, whose son, Ian, was also leaving to fight alongside the king. Though the king's army eventually rid Byland of its enemies, Erik and Ian never returned.

Quinn's family was gone.

Again.

Although Judith and Henry continued to care for him, their relationship lacked connection. They were kind and treated him well, but there was no warmth, no bond. It was as if every time the grief-stricken parents looked at Quinn, they were reminded of the son they had lost. Though they cared for his needs, they could never fully open their hearts to Quinn. For them, he represented the loss they had endured, the son they would never see again. For them, the pain was just too great.

Quinn felt the pain of loss as well, and an emptiness grew within his heart. Seeing his friends go home each day to the outstretched arms of their loving parents was a constant reminder of what he had lost, of the family he longed for.

He spent most nights fighting back tears until sleep and dreams came – dreams of soft laughter floating on a cool breeze. Dreams of lying on his back in a meadow, staring up at the clouds. Clouds shaped like the fading memories of the faces of his mother, his father, and his uncle.

During his waking hours, Quinn would often find himself daydreaming. He had never been more than a mile outside his village, and he wondered what lay beyond the edge of their small community, out in the vast kingdom of Byland. He spent hours imagining the possible adventures that awaited him if he ever had the chance to explore the outside world.

Little did he know his life was about to change.

An Unexpected Visitor

One day just after noon, a lone horseman rode down the dusty trail leading into the village. After being greeted by Tag, the town's blacksmith, the rider dismounted his muscled horse and asked for a drink of water. Tag quickly sent one of his apprentices to fetch the weary traveler something to quench his thirst.

While the water was being drawn from the well, a crowd of curious villagers, including Quinn, began to gather. The community wasn't used to visitors. The mystery man, though dirty from his travels, had a distinguished look about him. His dark hair hung to his shoulders, and his face was clean-shaven. He was dressed in garments suited for royalty. His britches were dark brown, his cloak forest green, and fastened to his belt was a sword. Quinn wondered if the man had ever used it in battle.

When his water arrived, the thirsty visitor drank it down as if his throat hadn't seen liquid for days. After politely asking for another cup and downing it as quickly as the first, he wiped his mouth with the back of his gloved hand and cleared his throat. The murmurs of the crowd, now made up of nearly half the village, died down.

"Greetings, citizens of Byland!" he began. "I am Nathaniel, and I thank you for your hospitality." The man's voice was noble and confident, just like his appearance.

"For the last few weeks, messengers like me have been traveling throughout the kingdom with a message." He paused to make sure he had everyone's attention. He most certainly did – everyone's gaze was fixed upon him.

"A message from the king."

At this announcement, the crowd began buzzing with excitement.

"A message from the king?" an old woman whispered to a friend. "What could it be?" Similar comments trickled through the gathering.

Quinn was thinking the same thing. *It must be important*, he thought.

After raising his arms for silence, the king's messenger reached into his cloak and pulled out a small, rolled-up piece of parchment. After slowly unrolling the small scroll, he again cleared his throat and began reading.

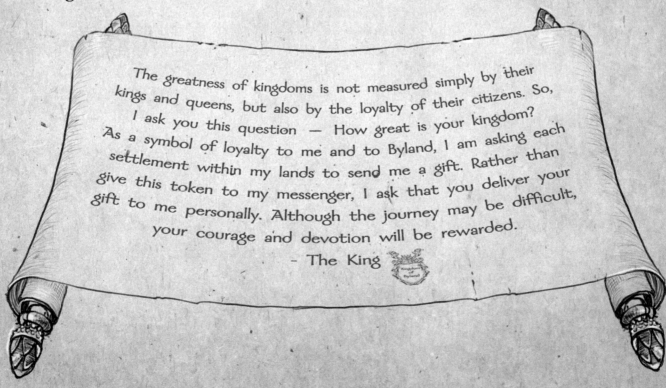

The greatness of kingdoms is not measured simply by their kings and queens, but also by the loyalty of their citizens. So, I ask you this question — How great is your kingdom? As a symbol of loyalty to me and to Byland, I am asking each settlement within my lands to send me a gift. Rather than give this token to my messenger, I ask that you deliver your gift to me personally. Although the journey may be difficult, your courage and devotion will be rewarded.

- The King

As soon as the messenger finished reading, everyone started talking at once.

"A gift?" said a woman under her breath.

"What does our village have that's worthy of presenting to the king?" asked Tag to his wife who had joined him.

"And who will take this gift?" she responded. No one even noticed the king's man as he replaced the scroll in his cloak, remounted his horse, and rode off.

I wonder who will go, Quinn thought. *What if I could make the journey?* His stomach began churning with excitement at the thought. *No, don't be silly!* he scolded himself. But he couldn't help it, and his imagination overtook him. As he walked back to Judith and Henry's to eat lunch and finish up his chores, a smile crept across his face as he pictured himself walking through distant lands, the king's castle on the horizon.

The Chosen

The next day, the town's leader named Aaron called all the villagers together to discuss the upcoming journey to the royal castle. There was an energy of expectation in the group that had gathered. Aaron stood on the back of a wagon and addressed the crowd.

"I have called you together to discuss the message we received yesterday. As I'm sure you all know by now, our king has asked that we bring him a gift." The crowd nodded, yesterday's visit from the messenger still fresh in everyone's mind. Aaron continued. "Now we must decide who will make this long and difficult journey. Do I have any volunteers?"

The hands of virtually every man, young and old, and even a few women, shot into the air. Shouts of "I will go!" and "It would be an honor!" rose from the crowd. Observing the sea of hands before him, Aaron grinned and slowly nodded his head. After a moment, he spoke again.

"Seeing so many of you willing to make the journey fills my heart with pride. I'm sure the king would be pleased." Aaron scanned the crowd, his face beaming. "Although each one of you would make a fine courier of our gift, we can't all abandon our village.

"I thought we might have a large number of volunteers, so I've come up with a way to choose." At that, he motioned to a burly man to his right. The huge man nodded and picked up a large black pot that was sitting on the ground before him. He moved toward the wagon and placed the iron container on the wooden cart at Aaron's feet.

"Thank you, my friend," Aaron said to the man. "In this cauldron," he continued, "are pieces of parchment, each containing the name of every able-bodied man in our village. I suggest we draw four names from the pot and these four people take *this*, our gift, to the king."

With that, he pulled from his cloak a small silver goblet and held it up before the crowd. A chorus of *oohs* rose from the gathered villagers.

"We are a small community with little wealth." Aaron said. "This cup is my family's most valuable possession, passed down to me from my father, who received it from his father. I am sure the king will be pleased with our gift." The villagers nodded in agreement, and several shouted their approval.

"So, what do you say? Shall we choose our cup bearers?" Aaron's question was met with raised fists and enthusiastic cheers.

Quinn's heart raced with anticipation as his mind filled with questions.

Is my name in the pot?

Am I "able-bodied?"

Am I even considered a man?

Aaron raised his arms for silence, and the excited murmurs of the crowd died down. The town's leader lowered his hands and held them out over either side of the iron cooking pot. He waited several seconds, as if to let the drama build, and then reached his hand into the old, rusty cauldron.

One by one, he slowly removed four pieces of paper, each containing the name of a chosen villager. He held the scraps high over his head so that all who were gathered could see. The crowd held its collective breath. Then he slowly lowered his arm and in a loud voice started reading the names.

"Thomas!" he boomed. Congratulations broke out around a man toward the back of the crowd.

"Graydon!" Aaron continued. A similar reaction just a few people to the left of Quinn.

"William!" Quinn barely noticed where the third lucky villager was standing, because his concentration was solely on Aaron, his gaze almost willing his name to be called.

Please, let him read my name, Quinn prayed silently. *Please.*

"And..." Aaron said, looking down at the final scrap of parchment. "Jonathan."

Quinn's heart sank. His shoulders sagged.

To his left, villagers started congratulating a middle-aged man, slapping him on the back. But the man was shaking his head and waving them off.

Seeing the man's reaction, Aaron asked, "Jonathan, what's the matter?"

"While I would be honored to help bring our gift to the king," Jonathan said, "my back is acting up again." He grimaced and placed both his hands on his lower back. "I don't think I'm fit to make the journey. Go ahead and select another name."

"Are you sure?" Aaron asked. Jonathan nodded. "Very well," Aaron said.

Hope rekindled inside Quinn's heart. There was still a chance!

Aaron again reached into the pot and pulled out another piece of paper. "And joining Thomas, Graydon, and William will be..." He looked down at the parchment. He paused and a smile crept across his face.

But Quinn didn't notice. His eyes were now closed.

"Quinn!" Aaron exclaimed.

A gasp rose from the crowd. Quinn opened his eyes. Had he heard correctly? Did he just hear his own name? He looked around and saw everyone smiling at him. He was going to see the king!

"Congratulations, Thomas, Graydon, William, and Quinn!" Aaron announced over the now-buzzing crowd. "Since we don't want to keep our king waiting, you will begin your journey tomorrow morning. Godspeed!"

A few of the villagers voiced concern that Quinn was too young to make the journey, but Aaron convinced them that Quinn would be more than safe traveling in the company of three strong men.

So, more excited than he had been in his entire life, Quinn ran home to pack. After stuffing his meager belongings into a small sack, he decided to lie down and get some sleep. He knew he would need all his energy for the adventure that awaited him. For a while, however, he just lay there, staring at the ceiling, excitement coursing through his veins. Eventually, he nodded off, but that night he dreamed a new and different dream.

He dreamed of a castle.

He dreamed of a man on a throne.

The Journey Begins

Early the next morning, the entire village rose at dawn to send off Quinn and his three companions. They carried with them the king's gift – the small silver cup. Since Quinn had the fewest supplies, his elders gave him the honor of carrying the small treasure in his pack.

The weather was comfortable, and the travelers enjoyed the beautiful scenery as they walked. Quinn took it all in, savoring every minute. For three days the villagers traveled over hills, through valleys, and across streams until one afternoon they approached a large forest. The group stopped and looked at the enormous obstacle that lay before them. The path on which they had been walking seemed to disappear into the darkness of the trees ahead of them.

There's something about those trees, Quinn thought. They gave him an uneasy feeling. He couldn't put his finger on it, but they seemed almost...alive. The sun, which until now seemed ever-present, appeared to dim. The wind began to blow, and a chill traveled down Quinn's spine.

"I've heard stories about this forest," said Thomas, his voice a little less bold than usual, his face turning pale. "Some say it's haunted."

"Haunted?" said Quinn in a shaky voice.

"Don't pay him any mind, lad," said Graydon, placing a hand on Quinn's shoulder. "He's just trying to scare you."

Well, he's doing a pretty good job, Quinn thought. He looked over at Thomas. The large man didn't look like he was trying to be funny.

"Well," Graydon continued, "I don't want to stop here. We have plenty of daylight left. Come on, let's get through the forest before nightfall."

With that, the four resumed walking down the path leading into the trees.

Be brave, Quinn told himself. *The forest isn't haunted. Those are just stories.*

As soon as they entered the thick rows of trees, the sunlight vanished, eclipsed by the huge canopy overhead. Graydon immediately told the three villagers to take out their lanterns and light them. With a beacon of light now before each of them, the group continued creeping along the forest path. A breeze again began to blow through the trees, making eerie sounds that caused the villagers to halt in their tracks.

"This place is haunted, I tell you," whispered Thomas, fear in his voice. His lantern illuminated the terror on his face.

The shifting shadows cast by the four glowing lanterns made it seem as if the tree branches were actually long, twisted arms, reaching out to grab the unsuspecting travelers.

Quinn was afraid. "Just keep looking forward," he whispered to himself. "It's only your imagination."

The group marched on, Graydon in the lead, followed by William, Quinn, and then Thomas.

As the path curved around a large tree, Thomas accidentally bumped into an outstretched branch. Thinking someone had grabbed him, he let out a scream.

"Haunted! This place is haunted!" he shrieked, jumping around as if trying to shake a hundred invisible spiders from his back. "The trees are alive! We have to turn back! We'll never make it through this cursed forest!"

Quinn, Graydon, and William turned to see their panicked companion running down the path back toward their village until he disappeared into the darkness. Graydon called out for Thomas to stop, but his frightened friend was already gone.

The three villagers stared down the now-empty path. Quinn wondered where Thomas would go and what would happen to him. Then he wondered what would happen to the rest of them.

After a few moments, Graydon broke the silence. "Well, I guess it's just the three of us now. Let's keep moving."

So, on they marched. The wind, now sounding like faint voices, continued to blow through the trees. Quinn began to tremble with fear, but he kept moving.

This will soon be over, he told himself. *Soon, I'm going to see the king.*

After what seemed like an eternity, the forest thinned, and the three villagers emerged from the trees just as the sun was setting. Exhausted both physically and mentally, they set up camp by a large boulder and used it to shelter themselves from the wind. After a meal of dried meat, cheese, and biscuits, the three spread themselves out under blankets on the grassy earth to get some sleep. In a few minutes, the only sounds that could be heard were the contented snores of the three weary travelers.

The Bridge

Quinn was roused early the next morning by Graydon who had already begun breaking down camp. When all their supplies were back in their packs, they continued on their journey. They walked at a good pace, stopping occasionally to quench their thirst by a stream and have a bite to eat.

For two uneventful days they walked, the path becoming a bit more rugged and steep. Late in the second afternoon, the party approached something that forced them to halt.

Up until this point, the trail had been fairly wide. Now it narrowed to only a few feet across. Then it stopped. Before them was an enormous ravine. Stretching across the gorge was a bridge made of old ropes and decaying pieces of wood. The rotting boards were laid side by side onto two parallel strips of rope stretching from one side of the ravine to the other. There were several spots along the bridge where pieces of wood were missing. About three feet above the bridge were two more lengths of fraying rope, seemingly there to hold onto when crossing.

Quinn carefully moved to the edge of the cliff and peered down into the ravine. Both sides were very steep, practically vertical, and the bottom was a long way down. Jagged rocks lined the canyon floor.

How are we going to get across? wondered Quinn. *I sure hope we don't have to use this bridge.*

Almost immediately after the thought had crossed Quinn's mind, Graydon spoke up. "Well, it looks like the only way to get across is this bridge. It's not the sturdiest thing I've ever seen, but I'm sure it will hold."

"Why don't we test it first," suggested William, who up until this point had been silent nearly the entire journey. He had walked up to the edge of the bridge, a skeptical look on his face.

"Good idea," said Graydon. He scanned the ground and picked up a rock about the size of his fist. He moved toward the bridge and gently tossed the stone onto one of the boards. The piece of wood split like a dry leaf and fell with the rock to the bottom of the canyon.

It was several seconds before anyone said anything, all three villagers staring silently down into the ravine. Finally, Graydon said, "Well, the rest of the boards seem much sturdier than that. If we're careful, I'm sure we can make it across."

"Are...are you sure?" asked Quinn in a shaky voice.

"Of course," Graydon responded, but his voice lacked its usual confidence.

Suddenly, William spoke up. "I'll go first." He tried to sound brave but didn't do a very good job. Quinn was surprised and relieved that William had volunteered to be the first to cross the rickety bridge. Now he wouldn't have to go first.

Gathering his courage, William slowly stepped forward and approached the bridge. Taking a deep breath, he cautiously put his hands on the side ropes and took a hesitant step out onto the bridge.

As soon as he put his weight onto the first wooden plank, it snapped in two! His foot plunged into the empty space where the board had just been, and William started to fall through the hole. Fortunately, he was still holding onto the hand ropes and caught himself from falling any further. Graydon leaped forward and struggled to pull William from the now-swaying bridge.

Once back on the ground several feet from the edge of the ravine, the two men collapsed. William, feeling solid earth beneath him, just lay there for several moments breathing heavily, the rest of his body paralyzed with fear. Finally, he rose to his feet and spoke.

"I won't go any further," he panted. "First, it was the forest. Now, it's this...this...*bridge*!" he said, motioning with his hand toward the frail rope and wooden structure. With that, he picked up his pack and started walking back the way they'd come.

"William, wait!" Graydon called, quickly rising to his feet and moving toward his friend. "Sit and rest a while." But William just waved Graydon off, ignoring his pleas to stay, and continued walking. After a few minutes, he disappeared over the horizon.

The two remaining villagers stood in silence for several seconds, staring in the direction William had gone. Then Graydon turned and walked back to the edge of the canyon. Quinn followed and asked, "What are we going to do now?"

"We don't have much of a choice," Graydon sighed after a moment. "We have to try and cross this bridge."

Another long pause.

"I'll go first," Graydon said. He then turned and bent down to meet Quinn's eyes, a serious look in his own. "Pay close attention to where I step," Graydon said, stamping out each word.

Then he turned to face the ravine and slowly approached the bridge. After a few moments of surveying the wooden planks and what appeared to be silent praying, Graydon gently stepped out onto the bridge.

As if walking upon a frozen lake, Graydon cautiously moved across the bridge, testing each step by putting a little weight on the next plank to see if it would support him. Quinn was unable to take his eyes off Graydon. He suddenly realized he was holding his breath and exhaled.

"Please make it across," he whispered to himself.

Although the bridge creaked, swayed, and twice lost planks that could not support Graydon's full weight, it served its purpose. After what seemed like an eternity, Graydon took a final step and planted his feet on the other side of the canyon. It looked like he too had been holding his breath, because he let out a huge sigh Quinn could see if not hear from where he was standing.

Once his feet were sure they could trust the ground upon which he stood, Graydon turned and faced Quinn. Cupping his hands to his mouth, he yelled back across the canyon. "Alright, Quinn! Now it's your turn! Go very slowly and remember to step where I stepped!"

Quinn swallowed hard and took a few steps toward the bridge. He put his head down, closed his eyes, and breathed deeply. *Don't worry,* he thought. *If Graydon can do it, so can I.* He stood still for a few more moments. *All right, let's go. The king is waiting for us.*

It was that last thought that gave him courage. The king was waiting for him. He *had* to make it across!

As his fear began to melt away, Quinn stepped out onto the bridge. Placing his feet only on the planks with Graydon's dusty footprints upon them, he slowly made his way across the bridge.

When he was halfway across, the wind, which until then had been perfectly calm, suddenly began to blow. The bridge started to sway. Quinn froze, his grip on the side ropes tightening.

"You're almost there!" came a reassuring yell from Graydon. Without moving his head, for the ability to move his limbs had seemed to desert him, Quinn raised his eyes toward his companion. "Just a few more steps!" Graydon added, an encouraging smile on his face.

Quinn lowered his eyes. The breeze died down a bit, and he regained control of his arms and legs. Although he moved much more slowly, he was able to cross the rest of the bridge without any missteps or broken planks. When he reached the other side he fell to his knees, looked to the sky, and mouthed the words *thank you*.

As nightfall was fast approaching, the two decided to call it a day and make camp. After a small meal, the tired villagers stretched out under the stars to get some sleep. And on that night, Quinn dreamed of solid, sturdy ground, a subject that would have seemed odd on any other night.

The Fork in the Road

Quinn and Graydon slept like babies. Perfect weather greeted them the next morning as they woke, broke camp, and continued on their journey. As they walked, they soaked in the beautiful scenery that made the hours fly by.

Late in the afternoon, Quinn noticed something shining far off in the distance. As they drew closer, the glistening object grew larger and began to take shape. It was an enormous castle sitting atop a large hill.

"There it is!" Quinn cried out. "The royal castle! We made it, Graydon! We made it!"

"Yes, we did, Quinn. Yes, we did," Graydon said triumphantly, his hands on his hips.

The two villagers continued walking along the well-traveled path until it led them to the foot of the hill. Standing at its base, it now looked more like a mountain.

It was here that the path forked. To the left, it continued much as it had up until this point, the ground even and relatively smooth. To the right the path led to the base of the steep hill. Quinn followed the trail with his eyes.

Unlike the road on which they had been walking, this path was littered with rocks and didn't look very inviting. It grew steeper and steeper until it seemed to disappear farther up the hill. Quinn then turned his eyes to the path that branched to the left. It, on the other hand, remained flat and even widened. It was free of any obstacles and seemed to curve around the mountain.

Quinn was just about to suggest they take the wider path when he noticed a small sign at the fork in the road. He had been so excited about seeing the castle for the first time that he hadn't even noticed it. Graydon walked over and eyed the small signpost. It was old and weathered, but its message was clearly legible. It read "Castle of Byland" with an arrow pointing to the right.

In the direction of the steep, rocky, uphill path.

Quinn's heart dropped. *That path?* he thought. He wasn't thrilled about the idea of tackling the rough, uphill trail in the fading daylight. He was just about to say as much when Graydon said, "This must be a mistake. That's hardly a path at all."

Quinn wasn't sure what to think. The uphill path did seem dangerous, while the other trail seemed safe and easy. While the rough route seemed to fade in the distance, the other grew larger, and was even lined with large maple trees. Still, Quinn had an unexplainable feeling that they should follow the sign's direction.

"I don't know, Graydon," Quinn said tentatively. "The sign says to go this way," he said, pointing up the hill to the right. "Why would the sign be wrong?"

Graydon sighed. "It's probably some kind of trick. Looks like someone is trying to lead us astray," he responded shortly. "If we take *that* path," he continued, rolling his eyes, "we will probably discover it ends halfway up the mountain and have to come all the way back down. It would be a waste of our time. Besides, it's getting dark."

He was right. The sun was beginning to dip below the horizon.

But the feeling in Quinn's heart didn't go away. It actually grew stronger. Before he knew what he had done, he blurted out, "I'm going up the hill."

Graydon slowly turned and looked at Quinn with raised eyebrows. Figuring the damage had already been done, Quinn continued. "The castle is on top of the hill, and this path leads to the top. Or at least I think it does. The sign says this is the way, and I believe it is." Quinn took a step back and waited for what he expected to be an angry response.

Graydon just stood there for a moment, a look of *I don't have time for this* on his face. He shook his head. "I'm going *this* way," he said, pointing at the path to the left. "I'll bet this path circles around the mountain and leads directly to the castle. I am *not*," he said, pounding a closed fist into the palm of his other hand, emphasizing the word *not*, "going to waste my time wandering the hillside in the dark. You can choose to come with me or not, but I'm going this way." With that, he started off down the left-hand path.

Quinn watched as Graydon turned and began walking away from him. His first instinct was to run and catch up with Graydon, but his legs wouldn't move. A determination in his heart, stronger than he'd ever felt before, held him where he was.

After about 20 strides, Graydon stopped and turned back to Quinn. "Are you coming?" he called back impatiently.

Quinn's mind screamed for him to run toward the man. But once again, his body wouldn't move, his heart's resolve fixing his feet to the ground. He just stood there and stared down the path, at his only remaining companion. The companion who was walking away.

And still his body wouldn't move.

After a few heartbeats, Graydon shrugged his shoulders, slowly shook his head, and said, "Suit yourself. I'll see you at the castle." He then turned back toward the path, continued walking, and in a few moments disappeared around the bend.

And just like that, Quinn was alone.

Though he felt a bit frightened being all by himself, he was also overcome with a surprising sense of confidence, a feeling that he had made the right decision, that everything was going to be okay.

He regained the ability to move his feet and turned to face the path before him. Shifting his gaze to the top of the hill, he could faintly see the castle's walls in the remaining traces of sunlight. He pulled the lantern out of his pack, lit it, and started up the trail.

The Castle

It was almost completely dark now. Quinn held the lantern out before him to try and light his way, but he was only able to see a few feet in front of him. As it grew darker, his fear grew deeper.

Maybe I should turn back, he thought. *Maybe Graydon was right.*

But every time a hint of doubt crept into his mind, the feeling in his heart overpowered it. *This is the right way,* his heart seemed to whisper. *Keep going. Your faith will be rewarded.*

So, on he went. Over cracks and around rocks he walked. The higher he climbed, the harder the path was to follow. But surprisingly, the rougher the trail, the more his lantern seemed to light his way. After about half an hour, Quinn reached the top of the hill and the ground leveled off.

Stopping to catch his breath, he looked around. The narrow and ragged trail he'd been following now merged into a wide, paved road. Catching a twinkle out of the corner of his eye, Quinn passed his lantern near the road to examine it more closely.

Could it be?

Dropping to a knee, Quinn brought his eyes and lantern to within a foot of the road. It was gold! *This must be the King's Highway!* he thought.

Quinn had heard some of the older folks in his village tell tales of a golden road leading to the royal castle, but he always thought they were just stories to entertain children.

His heart now pounding with excitement, Quinn popped back to his feet and hurried down the golden path, ignoring his exhaustion from the day's travels. A few minutes later, he came to the top of a small rise in the road and stopped. Before him stood the king's castle, an immense fortress larger than Quinn had even imagined. Its walls must have been thirty feet high, and its turrets and spires seemed to stretch endlessly toward the heavens.

With a sense of awe, Quinn approached the front gate. A man clothed in forest green emerged out of a small structure to the left of the gate. He slowly approached Quinn, his face hard. "May I help you, young sir?" asked the guard in a stern voice.

"Yes," answered Quinn, his voice cracking. "My...my name is Quinn. My village received a message from the king. I've come to bring him a gift."

The guard's face instantly softened.

"Please, excuse my rudeness, Quinn," the man said. "My name is Andrew. Please, follow me."

The two approached the gate, and Andrew left Quinn for a moment to speak with another guard. Andrew leaned close and whispered something in the second guard's ear. The man glanced up at Quinn with raised eyebrows. Then he disappeared through a door by the gate and a few seconds later, the gate rumbled and slowly opened. With a gesture from Andrew, Quinn was led into the castle.

A
Gift Given

Quinn's eyes became like saucers. The inside of the castle was more impressive than the outside! Andrew led Quinn into an enormous hall filled with beautiful artwork and tapestries. Countless candles and huge fireplaces on opposite sides of the room gave it a warm and comfortable glow. Andrew guided the awestruck boy through three similar rooms before the guard stopped before a large oak door.

"Please wait here while I approach the king," he said. He then bowed, opened the door, and disappeared into the room behind it, closing the door behind him. Quinn was left alone with his thoughts.

The king is on the other side of this door! he thought, nervous excitement coursing through his veins. *I'm finally going to see the king!* He wondered how many other subjects had already arrived to bring their gifts. A few moments later, the door opened, and Andrew reappeared.

"The king will see you now," the guard said with a smile and motioned Quinn toward the door.

Expecting to walk into a room filled with people, Quinn was surprised when the door closed behind him. The room was large but not decorated like the others he had seen upon entering the castle. Fireplaces on either side of the room provided a warm glow.

But the room was empty of people, except one. Opposite the door, some thirty paces away, was a large throne. On it sat the king.

He wore a burgundy robe with light brown cuffs and a golden crown. His hair was dark and his beard finely trimmed. He was everything Quinn had imagined a king should look like.

The boy nervously approached the throne, dropped to one knee, and bowed before the king.

"It's an honor to meet you, Your Majesty," Quinn said timidly.

"Rise, young one," the king said, his voice commanding yet gentle at the same time. "What is your name?"

Quinn's heart was pounding. Opening his mouth to answer, he found that his ability to speak was something he could no longer do without thinking. He had to concentrate to get the words out. "My name is Quinn, my Lord," he said finally. "I've brought you a gift from my village." He reached into his pack, removed the small silver cup, and handed it to the king. The king extended his strong hands and received the gift. Eyeing it, he smiled.

"Thank you, Quinn," the king said, setting the cup on a small table next to his throne. Then he turned back to Quinn and continued. "You must have traveled a great distance. Did you come alone?"

"No, my Lord. I set out with three companions." Quinn wondered what had become of Graydon and where his path had led him.

Quinn went on to tell the king about his journey – the forest, the ravine, the fork in the road, and how each man had made the decision to turn back or go his own way. The king sat and listened patiently.

"You are very brave to come so far, especially considering your friends left you," the king said when Quinn had finished. "Unfortunately, you've had to learn the hard lesson that not all friends will stand by you when things get tough."

Quinn frowned and nodded his head slightly.

The king continued. "You must have been frightened."

"I was, Your Majesty. But...but...never mind. It's silly," Quinn muttered, dropping his head in embarrassment.

"What? What were you going to say?" the king asked, leaning forward and clearly interested.

"Well," Quinn responded, looking up. "Every time I felt like giving up, a strange feeling in my heart seemed to push me to go on. I can't explain it, but...I knew you wouldn't have asked us to make a journey that wasn't possible to make."

The king sat back and smiled broadly. "Quinn, you have a faith that men many times your age do not possess," he said. Then he rose from his throne, stepped down, and stood in front of Quinn. After a moment, he said, "I sent the message you received to every village in the kingdom. Do you know how many gifts I have received?"

Quinn shook his head.

The king held up a single finger. "One."

He then turned around, walked back up the steps to retrieve the small cup from the table, and returned to Quinn. "You are the *only* one who has answered my request."

Quinn was shocked. *The only one? How could that be?* His surprise then turned to embarrassment. "I'm sorry it's such a small gift, my Lord. Our village is humble, and it was the most valuable thing we had." Quinn hung his head and his shoulders slumped.

The king reached out his hand, placed his fingers under Quinn's chin, and raised his head. "I care not about the gift, Quinn, but the giver," the king said in a soothing voice, his eyes fixed on Quinn's. "What you brought me is not important. What's important is that you chose to bring it."

The king took a few steps to his right, stopped, and then faced Quinn again. "My purpose in sending a message to every village was not to receive gifts. I don't have any need for more wealth." The king paused and took a step toward Quinn. "I wanted to see who had the courage and faith to honor me, not with gifts, but with trust and devotion. You, Quinn, have shown me these things."

Quinn's face flushed with pride. He had never imagined that he, a simple boy, could please the king. Yet here he was, standing in front of the most powerful man in the land, a man who just told him he had shown great courage. It was a dream come true!

The silence was broken when the king asked, "Tell me, Quinn. Why didn't your parents come with you?"

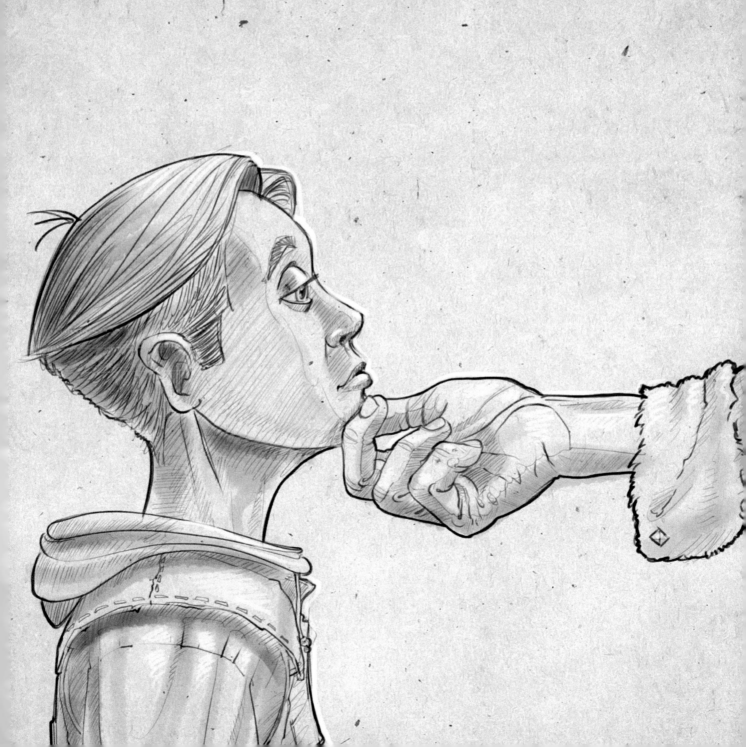

The joy Quinn had been feeling was quickly replaced by sorrow that accompanied the sudden reminder of his sad family history.

"My parents died when I was three, my Lord," Quinn said sadly, dropping his head once more. "My Uncle Erik raised me after that, but he was killed during the war."

He went on to explain how Judith and Henry had been taking care of him, but how they too lost their son in the war. Looking back up, he finished by saying, "They're nice enough, but I think I just remind them that they'll never see their son again."

"I see," the king said in a soft voice. "I am truly sorry." He sighed and then tilted his head back. "You said your uncle's name was Erik?" Quinn nodded. The king returned to his throne, sat down, and continued.

"Hmm. I remember fighting with a man named Erik during the war. What did your uncle look like?" After Quinn had described Erik, the king nodded, a look of recognition spreading across his face. "Ah, yes. The man you described is who I remember. He was truly a man of courage. I can see where you get yours." The king winked, and Quinn gave an embarrassed smile.

For several moments, the king said nothing. He seemed to be recalling the events of the war. Coming out of his daze, he looked at Quinn and asked, "Do you know how your uncle died?"

"No, Your Majesty," Quinn responded softly, sadness now clouding his face. He had heard nothing of his uncle's death, just that he was gone.

"Your uncle died saving my life," the king said.

Quinn's head jerked up. "Really?"

"Yes," the king replied. "He sacrificed his life to save mine. During one of the battles, he threw himself in front of an arrow intended for me." He paused, reliving the moment in his mind. Looking to the ceiling, his voice filled with emotion, he added, "He was one of the bravest men I've ever known."

Quinn couldn't believe what he was hearing. Erik had died saving the king's life! For a moment, his heart swelled with pride. But then reality quickly set in. This news didn't change the fact that his uncle was still gone. Quinn again hung his head.

The king looked down and saw the sad expression on Quinn's face. Then he looked into the distance as if he were thinking of something. After a few silent moments that seemed much longer, the king announced, "I have an idea. Joshua!" Instantly, a blond-haired man appeared at the door, dressed in the same fashion as the other castle guards.

"Yes, Your Majesty?" Joshua said.

"Would you please ask the queen to join me?"

"Right away, Sire." The guard turned and disappeared through the door.

The queen? Quinn thought, his eyes growing large. *I'm going to meet the queen!*

Several more minutes passed before the door reopened and through it walked the most beautiful woman Quinn had ever seen. She was dressed in a royal blue dress laced with gold. Her golden hair cascaded down her shoulders as she walked gracefully across the room to where the king sat. She leaned over and gave him a small kiss on the cheek. The king tilted his head and started whispering in the queen's ear. Quinn just stood there, nervousness growing inside him.

Finally, the queen straightened, lifted her head as if considering something, and nodded. Grinning, she turned toward Quinn.

"Welcome to our home, Quinn. I am so pleased to meet you," she said through her smile. Her voice was as beautiful as she was.

"Good evening, Your Highness," Quinn said bowing.

"Quinn, we have something we would like to discuss with you," the king said.

You do? Quinn thought.

"Yes, Your Majesty?" he said, totally confused as to what the king would need to talk with him about.

After a brief pause, the king said, "I don't know if you are aware, but the queen and I have no children."

Quinn's heart skipped a beat. His gaze shifted from the king to his wife. She wore a smile that would have warmed the room without the fireplaces.

The king continued. "Your uncle, though I knew him for only a short time, proved himself to be like a brother. He gave his life for me, and I will never forget his sacrifice." The king looked at his wife, then back at Quinn. "Quinn, it seems the queen and I have an opportunity to repay the debt we owe your uncle."

Quinn's heart was now pounding in his chest.

Is he...is he saying...what I think he's saying?

The king smiled and then asked, "Quinn, how would you like to live here with us in the castle?"

"My Lord?" Quinn said after a few seconds. He couldn't believe what he had just heard. It was like a dream.

"We would like you to stay here with us," the queen said. "We would like to adopt you, Quinn."

She stepped forward and placed her hands on his shoulders. "We know we could never take the place of your parents or your uncle, but we would love you with all our hearts as if you were our own."

Quinn's eyes filled with tears.

"Would you like that, Quinn?" the king asked, now standing beside the queen. "Would you like to become part of our family?"

Tears now streamed down Quinn's face.

"Yes!" he cried, jumping forward and throwing his arms around the king and queen. "I would like that very much!"

And so, Quinn's journey came to an end. He had set out to bring a gift to his king, never thinking he would receive one as well. One chapter of his life was now complete. A new and exciting one was about to begin.

THE END.

Discussion Questions

1. Which obstacle would have been the hardest for you to face:
    the forest, the bridge, or the fork in the road? Why?

2. Have you ever felt like Quinn, when you had to face something new or
    scary, but you didn't give up? What happened?

3. Quinn faced a difficult decision at the fork in the road when the right
    choice wasn't the easy one. When was a time you made a difficult decision
    but knew it was the right thing to do?

4. What do you think happened to Thomas, William, and Graydon?

5. What lesson do you think you can learn from this story?

Acknowledgements

In 1996, I had the opportunity to attend a presentation by award-winning children's book author Robert San Souci. As he spoke about the books he'd written and what inspired him to write, a fire was lit inside of me. I walked away thinking, *I want to do that. I want to write a children's book.* Mr. San Souci, thank you for your inspiration.

Johnny, thank you for taking my words and so beautifully transforming them into the works of art contained on the pages of this book. Never in my wildest dreams did I think I'd be able to work with an artist as talented as you. During our collaboration, your ability to consistently produce what was in my imagination was a joy. Thank you, my friend, for helping make this book happen!

Jill, my amazing wife, thank you for believing in me and consistently encouraging me to pursue my dream of making this book a reality. Your support over this 25-year journey has been invaluable. You've read and provided feedback on countless drafts, always encouraging me to keep going. This could not have happened without you. Thank you, Babe. I love you!

Meghan and Dad, my editors, thank you for lending me your time and expertise to help sharpen my literary sword. I will be forever grateful for your help in bringing my story to life in a way that is clear and, of course, grammatically correct. :)

Solomon Petchers, thank you for all your assistance in helping me navigate the path of self-publishing. Your support, encouragement, and sharing of your publishing experience have been so appreciated. Thanks, buddy!

And to all those who took the time to read and provide feedback on drafts of the story, thank you! Brian Butler, John Eick, Solomon Petchers, Stacy Allen, Cassie Lira, Monique Petrucci, Jeff Kubiak and Ann Kozma, thank you for playing an integral role in this journey. I greatly value your time, but more importantly, I treasure your friendship.

About the Author

Brent has been a teacher and administrator for over 25 years. He is also the author of *Stories of EduInfluence*, a collection of his real-life stories from the classroom and front office illustrating the life-changing power all educators possess. Brent and his wife live in Murrieta, California and are the proud parents of two adult children. For more information about Brent, visit his website at **brentcoley.com**.

About the Illustrator

Johnny is the Senior Creative Director of Storyland Studios, a design and production firm imagining, designing, and creating immersive experiences and environments that lift the spirit. Illustrating a children's book has always been on Johnny's bucket list, so working on *The Gift* has been a dream come true. For more information about Johnny, visit **storylandstudios.com**.